THE LOVE ILLUSION

BREAKING THROUGH THE BARRIERS OF CHRISTIAN DATING

Karen Maloy, Ed.S.

Mutual Blessings Books
Huntsville, AL
MBSuccess@karenmaloy.org
www.karenmaloy.org

Printed in the United States of America

Unless otherwise indicated, all Scripture quotations are taken from the New International Version of the Bible.
The Love Illusion: Breaking Through the Barriers of Christian Dating
Mutual Blessings Books
Publisher/Editor: MB Success Strategies
Published by Mutual Blessings - Huntsville, AL 35816
1-315-657-3648 - Website: **www.karenmaloy.org**

ISBN-13: **978-0-9856608-3-3**

DEDICATION

This book is dedicated to my children LaToya, Jemel, Myisha & Nyangel; my grandchildren Meishawn, Myshon, Marliah, Messiah, and Breasia; and my great-grandson Meishawn, Jr. May this book give you the guidance that you need to help you prepare yourself and your children to develop healthy, lifelong relationships

CONTENTS

Introduction

If you are like most Christians, you are confused about what to do about dating. You are tired of spending your time on relationships that start off okay, but over a period time they lose their luster and you end up with grief, heartache, and ill feelings that you carry onto your next relationship. Maybe you are frustrated because you are tired of waiting, or you don't know how to find that right individual for you. Perhaps you have been in a few serious relationships, only to find out that you wanted something more than they did; or maybe you are single again after being in a committed relationship, and are afraid of making the same mistakes again or choosing the wrong individual.

After having several unsuccessful relationships,

I can certainly say that I can feel your pain. There were many times that I was confused, and trying to date again using the world's system just did not seem appropriate for me as I was now a committed Christian. There were times that I actually prayed for God to send me someone who was ready for a serious relationship, or to please just take the desire away. I was so disheartened by the entire experience that I found myself getting angry with God, and I could not understand why He would allow me to desire something that I could not have.

During my dating experiences, I began to write down things that I thought would be helpful to other Christians in my same situation. I wanted to help teenagers, young adults, and single parents in their struggles, so that they could avoid some of the same mistakes that I have made. After several years, I have written several quotes, articles, and a book which I believe would be instrumental to anyone who is starting in what is commonly known as the *dating game*. Granted I am not an expert in dating; however, through dating and my own personal experiences, I believe that I at least have wisdom on what NOT to do!

Finally, I must say that I am now implementing these principles in my personal life, and they are not just theories. I am grateful that God did not answer my prayer to take away my desire for a suitable mate, for I am now saying that I am looking forward to the dating experience. I have utilized these guidelines to end fruitless relationships, and I will also be using them to *screen* all of my future prospects.

During this time in my life, I spend a great deal of time working with single women and mothers, and gleaning from my own personal experiences I am finding that there are some basic biblical principles which are fundamental for all relationships including dating relationships. I find that if we choose to date according to these guidelines, our relationships will be truly blessed. However, I also believe that if you choose to violate these principles you will also suffer the consequences of those decisions. I have decided to combine my own personal experiences with the information that I have gathered from my research, and this book "The Love Illusion: Breaking Through the Barriers of Christian Dating is the result.

My vision is that this book will provide you with some basic guidelines which would help you to avoid the problems associated with modern dating strategies, and to increase your odds of having a successful dating experience. In addition, this book could serve as a valuable resource for singles and youth ministries. I promise to stay away from the vague and confusing clichés which are often heard at single ministries and fellowships. This book will offer simple, practical advice on how to prepare oneself for dating, what to look for in a date, the difference between the date and a mate, what to avoid when looking for a mate, and most importantly how you can glorify God in your dating relationships. The truths that you find in this book will have a clear moral foundation based upon biblical principles. If you heed the advice which will be offered in this book, you may be able to protect yourself from the heartache and pain which is often associated with contemporary dating. These tools will provide the foundations that you need to present yourself as a suitable mate, and will help you to build a healthy, loving, and lasting relationship with another individual.

Now that we have discussed what we will cover in this book, there are a few things that we must address before we begin this process. If we do not address these concerns right now, they will only lead to further resistance to implementing these principles later.

Having deviated from God's original intent of morality, we have come to accept that what feels good is good for us. This creates considerable problems as we begin to think that God does not want us to enjoy our lives. The second concern lies in the area of patience. We now live in what I refer to as a *microwave* generation where we have to wait for very little. Many people get angry when they have to wait in line even for fast food.

I am reminded of a time when my oldest daughter informed me that the microwave was no longer working. At first I responded with "no problem" as we were planning to move within the next 30 days; however, that plan only lasted until the next evening. My original plan was to put off purchasing a new microwave for at least a few weeks; but that only lasted until the meal that I had cooked in the crock pot in the previous evening had to be heated up. I realized after 40 minutes that it was perhaps time to rethink that decision. The very next day I went out to purchase a microwave. It did not take me long to realize that I was not willing to *practice patience* in this area.

The world that God created is based upon the principle of *seedtime and harvest*. We just need to know that some things just take time, and the same is true for our relationships. The seed begins with our desire to share our lives with another individual; however, we must not forget the "time". Time must be invested before a harvest can be obtained. We will explore this ideology further in a later chapter.

I want you to seriously consider the principles which I am presenting in this book. I can suspect that addressing the confusion which arises from dating misconceptions will simply help you to avoid many of the mistakes made when dating. The principles discussed in this book are designed to show you how to uncover any wrong thinking patterns so you may be successful in your love life.

So what is dating? I am so glad that you are

seeking an answer to that question. Given that dating is the process which will lead you to one of the most important stages of your life, you cannot afford to ignore these principles. Written from a Christian perspective, this book is focused on the Christian audience; however, given that the material is also morally based, it is also a valuable resource if you are not a Christian.

The first section of this book will present a definition and a model for Christian dating. After that we will discuss the reason for dating, and what can and cannot be accomplished through the world's way of dating. Individual, parental and church responsibility concerning this subject are also discussed. I believe that if we can explore God's word further, we will find that although He does not tell us how to date, we can however find the principles which are invaluable in this stage of development. We can train our people in such a way that they can not only date safely and choose wiser dates, but they can ultimately date in a way which can increase their influence on society and change the future for the better.

As you begin this journey I pray that you will

develop a better understanding of God's intent for your life and a better understanding of yourself. In addition, I pray that the Spirit of Truth will reveal all it is that you need to know. It is only when this occurs can we truly say that we are ready for the dating experience.

Many things that we will explore will also begin to challenge what you have been taught, or what you already believe. If that should occur, I encourage you to confront your ideas surrounding this area. I also encourage you to seek God and ask Him about the plans that He has for your life. This will make a world of difference since He is the one who created you. I can assure you that He is all-knowing and will also know what will make you happy. Seeking His input in this area is not only necessary, but it will also determine your success in creating healthier relationships.

We know that negative consequences come from bad decisions, and this principle is valid no matter what your beliefs are. You may have already made these very mistakes in the past and are dealing with those consequences, but it is never too late to implement what is learned and start making better decisions in your present. I believe that if you follow these guidelines in all of your relationships, you will have more peace, more joy, and more satisfaction within your relationships. I encourage you to remember that the only one who can stop you from being successful is you, so why not do all that you can and take the next step toward success.

Section 1
Christian Dating:

Its Definition, Purpose, and Result

Wisdom Key

"Children are impacted as they grow up in broken and unhappy homes, and ultimately society is impacted as children grow up and fulfill the leadership roles within society."

Chapter 1

In the Beginning

There is nothing but confusion when we look at how an individual is supposed to date, and it is even more confusing if you are a Christian. The response received from a married individual is generally the same - "you just wait on God". Perhaps it is because they have already made their mistakes and hopefully have learned from them; or they may have gotten married for all of the wrong reasons. Maybe it was because they were pregnant and felt that they had to be responsible, or because they felt like they waited long enough and had no other options. Whatever the reasons that they got married, chances are when they started the dating process they had some of the same misconceptions as many other Christians, and lacked clarity surrounding the process as well. I am not saying that all people get married for the wrong reasons, for there are some people who felt like they got it right. They married because they were actually in love. However, I would like to explore further if love is really the primary reason in order to get married. If Christians are ever to develop a proper system of dating for the body of Christ, we have to go back and explore what God's original intent for relationships was when He created the world.

Now this is an interesting concept to explore. If we want to understand its purpose, we have to first discern the mind of God as it relates to dating. We have to ask two questions in which to begin (1) first is dating necessary, and (2) when did it become necessary. The answers lies in the bible beginning with Adam and Eve.

It must first be noted that the word "dating" does not exist in the bible, and neither does God provide any guidelines for it. With that being said, the Bible does have a lot to say about relationships, partnerships, and teamwork; and these terms will provide the foundational principles necessary for understanding how to have a successful dating relationship. For this reason I have found this definition to be the most effective to define Christian dating:

"It is the process by which individuals explore potential mates for the purpose of developing deeper relationships in preparation for marriage - a lifelong partnership".

With this definition in mind, the terms that we have identified as relationships, partnership, and teamwork will be used interchangeably throughout this book. We will begin with exploring the Bible to uncover answers to the previously mentioned questions about dating.

In Genesis 1, we find that God by creating Eve arranged the first marriage between man and woman. This is the pattern which we will see continued throughout the bible. This was evident in cultures of nobility where children were promised to each other to ensure alliances and treaties between countries, such as the marriage between King Solomon and Pharaoh's daughter. This also occurred with Abraham sending his steward Eliezer to find a wife for Isaac. The thing of most importance here is to realize that during the biblical era there was no need for dating as marital relationships were arranged. The responsibility for finding a suitable mate for the children rested with the parents. Throughout history women did not have the right to choose their husbands. In the current era of women's liberation, a young woman may even find this offensive as it takes away her right to choose. Given this history, I find it very hard to believe that you would find anyone who would want to have their parents arrange their marriages. However, taking into consideration the divorce rates in countries such as India,

Africa, and some countries which still adhere to this ancient principle, something is to be said for arranged marriages.

According to the Everything Engagement website, India has a divorce rate of 1.1 percent, and the United States and Canada has a divorce rate of 40-50%. While these numbers are inconclusive, it does not take a rocket scientist to figure out that the divorce rate when people have the right to choose has been pretty high.

Returning to the two questions that we are exploring about dating (is it necessary and when did it become necessary), we find that dating is necessary in today's culture, and it became necessary when arranged marriages stopped being the means for finding potential mates. Unfortunately Christians are no different than non-Christians when we consider statistics in the area of divorce rates. For this reason, it is plain for us to see that education in this area is necessary for the body of Christ. Only when we have the proper training and tools can future generations be taught how to avoid the many problems which are created from marrying the wrong individual.

When we look at the problems associated with marrying the wrong individuals, we must remember that marriage is not operating in a vacuum. All individuals involved in the relationship are impacted mentally, emotionally, physically, and spiritually; and this is most often associated with negative emotions.

Children are impacted as they grow up in broken and unhappy homes, and ultimately society is impacted as these individuals are the ones who grow and fulfill the leadership roles within our communities. As a result, we are currently experiencing high teenage pregnancy rates, increased instances of violence, and a decrease in morality. Children are now growing up in a depraved world which does not value life, much less the word of God. Christians cannot afford to fall prey to these worldly principles when it comes to educating our people in this area because too much is at stake. We must never forget that the only way to make right decisions is to rely solely on the word of God for guidance. As I have heard my Pastor Apostle Bret Wade say many times, "It is not who is right but, it is what is right". The word of God must once again become the place that we go to seek answers to the many questions we have in life. We must begin to base our very lives upon these very principles. So what exactly is the true purpose of dating for the Christian, and what does the term "Christian dating" really mean? These are just a few of the questions that we will seek to find an answer to. Having been a single mother who grow up in a single home, I am a perfect example of what happens when the proper guidance is not placed in a child while they are young. Proverbs 22:6 tells us to "train up a child". I can honestly say that I was trained in this area but, I was not taught in a godly manner. In addition, after serving as a Minister in a church, I have seen many single people grow despondent and impatient as they are waiting for their mate to find them in the church. I was one of them, and I must also add that I am a perfect example of what not to do! Many others eventually left the church never to be heard of again. It is for these reasons that I have developed an increased passion to find a way to help Christians to become successful in this area. As I have searched the Scriptures (and with the revelations I have received from my own experiences along the way), I have devised some biblical principles which I believe will help us. These principles I believe are at the heart of Christian dating.

1. Teaching how to date is the responsibility of the parents;

2. Dating must have a primary desire to please God;

3. Dating must be based on the bible being the absolute, infallible, undeniable, and incorruptible word of God;

4. The way we date must not hinder the development of our children spiritually or

morally; and

5.   We must know that dating has a divine purpose which proceeds beyond the now stage in our lives.

It is important that we consider these principles carefully, and ask God for a deeper understanding and revelation as we continue throughout this book. Remember that the purpose of this book is to (1) prepare you for a successful dating experience, and (2) to help you to approach this stage in your life with confidence.   The way that we approach our dating relationship will determine what it is that we end up with. If you are just looking for someone to have fun with, the chances of you finding someone who you can have fun with and rely upon is less than it would be if you were looking for someone with both of those qualities to begin with.

It is time that the body of Christ to give full attention to God's original plan for relationships. The future of the body of Christ will be influenced by how we choose to date, and who we choose to partner ourselves with. We can no longer afford to do things the way that we have been. We must be sure that we are doing everything that we can to ensure that individuals are learning how to date with principles which are established within the bible.

Wisdom Key

"What we have in us influences the type of people we associate with; it influences the things we do within our relationships; and it influences the decisions that we make that impacts our lives and the lives of those individuals we pour into."

Chapter 2

Defining Christian Dating

The term "Christian Dating" is not something that you
hear specified in the church today. Given that it is not
specified, I am not sure if anyone has a clear understanding of
what it means. Ben Young and Dr. Samuel Adams offer in
their book *10 Commandments of Dating* what they called "time
tested laws for building successful relationships". They
sought to help Christians to avoid the problems associated
with modern dating, and increase their chances of successful
dating by presenting practical and godly approaches to dating.
This served as a reminder that it is okay to date, but we must
also remember to consider and put God first in the
relationship. It is only by keeping Him in the relationship can
we avoid falling into the trap of "flesh". This was man's
original sin in the Garden of Eden as Adam and Eve chose to
give in to themselves and *their own desires*.

While many Christians will agree that our lives need to be guided by Godly principles; however, when it comes to our relationships many of us do not consult the bible to establish a plan on how to do it. Many of us spend more time and put more effort into planning our wedding ceremony then we would in planning our future, and it is our future which has the long-term consequences. When we ignore God's way on how to do these things, we are actually ignoring what it best for us because the bible clearly says that He has our best interest at heart.

> *For I know the plans I have for you," declares the LORD, "plans to prosper you and not to harm you, plans to give you hope and a future. Jeremiah 29:11*

Eve did not believe that God had her best interest at heart when she ate the *forbidden fruit*. At that moment she chose to believe that God was trying to keep something from her.

> *4 Then the serpent said to the woman, "You will not surely die. 5 For God knows that in the day you eat of it your eyes will be opened, and you will be like God, knowing good and evil." 6 So when the woman saw that the tree was good for food, that it was pleasant to the eyes, and a tree desirable to make one wise, she took of its fruit and ate. She also gave to her husband with her, and he ate. Genesis 3:4-6*

Unknowingly to Adam and Eve, God was trying to protect them (and the world) from the traps of Satan, and immediately upon eating the fruit (he was right) their eyes were opened, and their lives were changed forever. Adam and Eve now knew the truth, and although they wanted for things to return back to the way that it was before, unfortunately for them (and us) it was too late. This same principle holds true for us in our relationships. God's biblical principles are there to protect us from the dangers of making the wrong decisions. God is always trying to protect us from the emotional, mental, physical, and spiritual outcomes which result from us choosing the wrong mates; He is trying to protect our children from broken homes; and He is trying to protect society from immorality and depravity. He is trying to protect all of our futures.

The same situation that occurred with Adam and Eve in the Garden of Eden is occurring within Christian circles today. As we have turned away from God's hedge of protection, we are trying to do it our own way and control our own lives. As a result, we have been subjected to all of these things, and are now entering our perspective relationships with way too much "baggage". We want to call it wisdom that we have learned from our previous relationships, yet things such as distrust, dishonesty, manipulation, insecurity. low self-esteem, etc. are all things that we bring into our relationships, and whether we want to admit it or not, they all have negative consequences.

Failure to understand Christian dating has led to some

negative consequences within the Christian themselves, as well as in the body of Christ. Our children are no longer looking to the word of God or the church for answers; but, they are now exploring other avenues for answers to many of their questions. The influence of peer relationships as well as the internet and other social media, increases during the adolescent stage of development, and this is a very influential stage in their development. And let us not forget the problems associated with pornography and internet chat rooms on family relationships as well. This has led to a further decline as there is now a lack of commitment to one individual, as well as an increased depravity in our sexual experiences as well.

Consider what John Coblentz of Christian Family Living stated in 1992:

> *"God calls parents to be good teachers and children to be good learners so that they in turn can become good teachers of their children. This interaction between parents and children begins even before verbal communication is possible. It continues in one form or another throughout life. The responsibility of parents teaching their children is one which for certain learning situations can be delegated, but it can never be unshouldered. Children need the experience of learning from their parents; parents need the experience of learning from their children." (Basic Family Structure, Chap 1)*

Christians will agree that this is their responsibility as parents, and yet, how many can say that they are actually living out this responsibility? It is clear that the breakdown has occurred somewhere, but very few people will want to admit that they must assume part of the blame. It is clear that this problem did not occur overnight, but it is a problem which has been festering for generations. According to Glen Shultz who wrote *Kingdom Education* the problem lies in influence of postmodern philosophy. He wrote:

> *"Postmodernism states that there is no such thing as truth. Therefore, education serves the purpose of guiding students to create truth that is in accord with their individual belief systems... since all truth is created by individuals, then all truth must be equally valid. Therefore, postmodern thought tells us that there is no truth, only truths. There are no principles, only preferences."* *(Kingdom Education, p 27-28)*

What this tells us is that individuals are no longer relying on God's view to shape the decisions that they make for their lives. They are basing their decisions on what they want instead of what is right, and this will have negative consequences. This is what we are currently experiencing, as people are choosing what feels good as the sole purpose for the things they do, and as a result society is suffering. The consequences of individuals sowing to their flesh is evidenced by teenage pregnancies, increased violence, drugs and alcohol, etc. This has also had considerable impact on the church as we have also lost the irreverent fear of the Lord. While it is not impossible to reverse this negative trend, it cannot occur without true repentance and the re-education of the body of Christ. This will not be accomplished until Christians know, understand, and recommit their lives to living fully by the principles of God's laws.

In trying to develop a definition for Christian dating, I first had to explore God's purpose for marriage. The answer was found in Genesis 1:28:

> *God blessed them and said to them, "Be fruitful and increase in number; fill the earth and subdue it. Rule over the fish in the sea and the birds in the sky and over every living creature that moves on the ground. "*

God created man (and woman) to be fruitful, multiply, replenish, subdue, and have dominion. That means that our lives have a divine purpose which includes more than ourselves. Much like the tree is expected to bear fruit to satisfy our hunger, God wants us to do something to benefit the world in which we live in. Many of us accomplish this by using our gifts, talents, and abilities. This is the reason why God placed them within us even before we were formed in our mother's womb.

> *"Before I formed you in the womb I knew [a] you, before you were born I set you apart; I appointed you as a prophet to the nations. " Jeremiah 1:5*

They are to help us to fulfill our divine purpose on this earth. It is our divine destiny. Jesus understood that, and when the tree did not fulfill its purpose by bearing fruit, He cursed it.

> *The next day as they were leaving Bethany, Jesus was hungry. 13 Seeing in the distance a fig tree in leaf, he went to find out if it had any fruit. When he reached it, he found nothing but leaves, because it was not the season for figs. 14 Then he said to the tree, "May no one ever eat fruit from you again." And his disciples heard him say it. Mark 11:12-14.*

This scripture demonstrates to us that when we have done little with our lives we have nothing to offer back to society; and ultimately, our lives serve little purpose.

Next God expects us to multiply and reproduce ourselves. We can do that either literally by having babies and training them in the things of God, or we can accomplish that by pouring ourselves into others who are not our natural born children. In any event whether we are imparting godly or ungodly principles makes no difference, we are still pouring and reproducing ourselves into others. The same is true for replenishing, subduing, and having dominion, what we have in us influences what comes out of us.

In these verses God is telling us that we were created to operate in this manner. Therefore, when we think about dating we have to remember this principle. What we have in us influences the type of people we associate with; it influences the things we do within our relationships; and it influences the decisions that we make that impacts our lives and the lives of those individuals we pour into. It was from these truths that we arrive at the previously mentioned definition for Christian Dating.

In the definition previously mentioned, the basic fundamentals for dating from a biblical perspective is made with two implications (1) the first implication is that dating is founded upon the undeniable word of God which is the final authority; and (2) dating must be God-centered and God-focused. Based on this, there is no denying what is the truth and this will serve as the deal breaker in the midst of disagreements; and God must be in every area of your lives individually. This is necessary so that when you finally say "I do" to become one flesh, you both come together to create a household which is also God-centered. Kingdom principles must guide the entire process to provide the foundation necessary for successful relationship building and family development.

Wisdom Key

" Your purpose for dating is important as it determine the outcome."

Chapter 3

The End Result of Dating

The end result of dating should be obvious - it should be marriage. Unfortunately, for many Christians as they do not approach each of their dates from that perspective, they waste a great deal of time dating individuals who are not marriage material. Your purpose for dating is important as it will determine the outcome. For example, if you are looking for a date just so you can have fun together, then it does not make much sense for you to invest needless time in trying to find your areas of compatibility. On the other hand, if you are looking for a date in order to get married, then I would suggest you make sure that they are also marriage-minded desiring the same outcomes before you enter into the relationship.

It is every parent's desire that their children be successful in life; therefore, they have to do what they can to ensure that this happens. This could not occur however, if they do not have the information themselves. So where do parents get the information that they need so that they can train their children properly? Many of them were also taught and dated according to the same misguided principles and misconceptions that the world is now offering. While a Christian can obtain some level of competency by making a decision that they are not going to have sex before they get married, there is more to the process of dating. If Christians are not aware of this, they are still at considerable risk of choosing the wrong kind of mate. This is important because we must also remember that the individual that we choose to marry will also pour into the lives of our offspring. If the parents do not have healthy relationships, it is not beyond reason to assume that their children will not have healthy outcomes. Therefore, as Christians we should desire a relationship which is Christ-centered, continually evolving into the image of God, and focused on serving Christ in our daily lives (Schultz, 2007). To get a better understanding of how to do that, we must get a better understanding of the differences between a biblical-centered and a man-centered worldview.

- A view of the nature of God
- A view of the nature of man
- A view of knowledge

- A view of right and wrong
- A view of the future

As a man-centered and God-centered perspective can exist in each of these components, it is necessary for individuals to take the time to evaluate their view of each component to ensure that they have not fallen prey to man-centered perspectives as the result of any misconceptions.

Each individual is unique, and they bring to any environment their individual challenges. In spite of it all however, they have the responsibility to grow and mature intellectually and socially. Each individual is responsible for their own learning. Three elements which are essential to this process is (1) their desire to learn what God says; (2) mentors which challenge them to grow and learn, and (3) their own determination to learn. Ultimately, Christians must now seek answers on their own to establish a foundation for themselves, and finally to measure their relationships based upon the principles they discovered from their own search for truth.

There are two factors which determine what the outcomes from our relationships will be:

1.   What we believe to be the ultimate reality.
2.   What we believe to be the ultimate truth.

Unfortunately this is not what the world has taught us as educational institutions are no longer based upon what we believe to be absolute truth - the word of God. Our children are taught the theory of evolution as a belief, and this is certainly contrary to the word of God. This false ideology is widely accepted in schools, and has shaken the very foundation of God's supremacy as our creator. This further leads to the questioning of the idea of His word as the instruction manual of life, and finally disbelief in God himself. Our concepts of both of these aforementioned questions will determine who we place our hope in, what we place are values on, and will influence what we pass onto our children and those we pour into. Therefore Christian dating must have its foundations in God being the center of reality and his word as the ultimate authority.

The theory of evolution has had dire consequences on our children, and has had a negative impact on society. This theory has reduced man to being nothing more than a mere natural phenomenon, and we have now lost the meaning and value for life, including our own. How else can we explain the high instances of heart disease, high blood pressure, and high cholesterol? Obesity is another contributory factor and it is running rampant among our young people. This is a direct result of us not caring for our bodily temples.

We have already discussed the increase in violence but, suicide is also running rampant amongst our young people. Without a supreme being in which to place our hope in, many people are living in a world with no hope, and are finding that they really have no reason to live.

We should not be shocked to hear that our presidential candidates are in support of same sex marriages even though they say that they are Christians. Our sense of morality has been reduced to what is our preference and what we believe to be true, and this has also essentially devalued God's laws within society. In addition, we are also spending more time focusing on the end result, and less time focused on trying to understand why this is happening. We must once again redirect our focus on our belief system, and ensure that we are instilling godly values into our young children. By impacting this area of their lives we can ensure that they grow up to be adults who are morally and ethically sound, and who are prepared to become our future leaders who lead with integrity. After all, the children are our future. If we neglect to instill in them a biblical worldview, we fail to lay the groundwork for a moral society.

Start children off on the way they should go,
and even when they are old they will not turn from it. Proverbs
22:6

In summary, the body of Christ must understand that their beliefs will be determined by their worldview, and this is important because they will eventually act out of their beliefs.

"We must understand that our beliefs matter in life because:

- *what we believe determines our behavior;*
- *what we believe counts forever; and*
- *what we believe determines how we serve Christ." - Gary Schultz*

Section 2

Christian Dating:

Identifying The Problem

Wisdom Key

"Most treasures are buried beneath the surface, and they are never easy to get to either. Keeping this in mind, you must carefully screen each individual that presents themselves to you as a potential, and not just settle because you have been waiting for a long time."

Chapter 4

The Illusion

Now that we have a better understanding of God's original intent for mankind, created a definition for Christian dating, discussed the end result for dating, and the importance of wise counsel; we are now at the point where we can face the problem at hand. So what is the problem? I have come to the conclusion that the problem with Christian dating lies with the deception that I refer to as the *love illusion*.

Merriam-Webster's dictionary defines illusion as follows:

1   *a*   *obsolete*: the action of deceiving
     b (1) the state or fact of being intellectually
          deceived or misled;
     (2)   an instance of such deception
2   *a (1)* a misleading image presented to the vision
     (2)   something that deceives or misleads
          intellectually
     b (1) perception of something objectively
          existing in such a way as to cause
          misinterpretation of its actual nature

(2) HALLUCINATION
(3) a pattern capable of reversible perspective

Based on these definitions we can be sure of one thing - that an illusion is based on non-truths, conjectures, misconceptions and its intent is to mislead and deceive.

Every little girl grows up with the dream of meeting her prince, the one who will love and cherish her until death does her part, and I was no different. As I am not a male, I can only surmise that little boys grow up with the idea of becoming a women's Prince Charming. I grew up watching fairy tales like *Cinderella* and *Snow White*, and my children grew up with the movies *Beauty and the Beast* and *The Little Mermaid*. They were good, wholesome, and clean movies in which children and adults alike could enjoy. Unfortunately while its intentions were good, it failed to help me to develop a realistic view of what life, love, and relationships are all about. These movies only helped to shape a skewed and unrealistic view of the *perfect love relationship*.

How many of you have heard the following statement in church "You just wait on God and He will send you your mate"? While I am not saying that God cannot do that, what I am asking you to do is consider the following scripture.

Find *a good spouse, you* **find** *a good life— and even more: the favor of* GOD! *(MSG) Proverbs 18:22*

Christians we must understand how important this scripture

is for finding a mate, not only for men but also for women who are ready for the dating stage of their lives.

As I reflect upon my dating experiences, I recall sitting there and waiting every year for that perfect man to appear. There I was working and raising four young children on my own. I was also very active in ministry, and I was determined to do everything well. In order to achieve the goals that I had set myself, it was important that I did well in doing everything that I was instructed. In the beginning I took careful notes as to how to act, dress, and speak as a single woman. I attended every church service, participated in every church event, and took all the classes that my church informed me was necessary. Yet year after year as I kept waiting for the perfect man to appear, I realized that I was also getting more discouraged and despondent. Each single man that came into the church sent my heart into a state of utter chaos, fluttering from exhilarated anticipation, and fear as I was always afraid of another disappointment. These emotions were fighting with each other within me, as I wondered *"Is he the one"!* Is he the one who will make all of my dreams come true? Is he the one who will complete me? Is he the one who will take me away from this period of longing and loneliness? It would be years later before I realized that I had been like everyone else misguided by the *love illusion.* Does that mean that I had given up on love? Well of course not! However, I have now

43

realize that there is more to the process than the waiting.

Sitting in the church pew each week and listening to your Pastor preach to wait for your mate, is no different than me sitting on my front porch, and waiting for that man to come up to me and say "*I am the one created just for you!*" Sounds crazy doesn't it? Well, that is exactly what many of us have been taught to do. I found myself over ten years later sitting in the same place, still waiting, and getting more disheartened.

Another part of the illusion is believing that there is such a thing as a *perfect mate*, that there is someone that God has created specifically just for you to fit with you like a hand-in-glove. Consider the following statement from Dr. James Houran who is a respected expert in the psychology of compatibility:

> "*So, do these perfect partners exist? No, they don't. The term "soul mate" is poetic rather than scientific. Moreover, idealized notions of a perfect partner only reinforce unrealistic expectations people have when they search for a mate. James Houran, Ph.D"*
> *(Excerpted from Is there such as thing as soul mates?)*

While I do agree that there is no such thing as a perfect mate or a soul mate, I do subscribe to the belief that some people are more compatible for you than others. Unfortunately, this would also imply that there are some people who are less compatible with you than others as well.

A good and godly mate must be sought out, found, and discovered just like a treasure. If the treasure is left out in the open for all to see, it will not be there long enough for the right person to come along who deserves it. Most treasures are buried beneath the surface, and are never easy to get to. Keeping this in mind, you must carefully screen each individual that presents themselves to you as a potential, and not just settle because you have been waiting for a long time. Lord knows that I have made that mistake many times. There is a consequence for violating this principle. It is called chaos, confusion, heartache, grief, and much pain. Just like you must prepare yourselves to be a treasure, you must also be equally schooled on how to recognize a treasure. If you do not remember anything else in this book, I encourage you to remember this - not everything that looks good is good, and not everything that glitters is gold! Much like the tactics that Satan used to deceive Eve, he will most certainly use another individual to get you off focus, and then ultimately get you to disobey God's principles.

Like many of you who are finding themselves reading this book, each passing year grew increasingly worst weighing heavily on my heart. I can recall many nights crying myself to sleep, and crying out to God asking him "Why?" I remember how much it hurt to see even the sinner walking the street with someone, and there I was ten years later - still waiting. It would not be until years later that I would finally understand. God's answer to me regarding my singleness was not attributed to one single thing but a combination of many.

First I must note that ascribing to the belief of a soul mate, I was looking for that perfect individual that we would fit together like *hand-in-glove*. For this reason, if I had met a good mate for me, I probably would not have recognized him anyway. Secondly, I had done nothing to prepare for a mate; and even worst yet, I had not even determined why I wanted a mate. What I did not understand is how the end goal determined the basis of the relationship. For example, if the end goal is to find someone to have fun with, and not to get married, then be honest enough to share that information with the individual that you are dating. If they have that information, then they are at least in a position to make a wise decision regarding pursuing a relationship with you. Consequently, if the end goal is to get married, then you do not want to waste any time dating individuals who have demonstrated that they do not want to get married. It is sad when one pursues an individual thinking they are going to be the one to change them. Forget it! If they are not ready when they met you, they did nothing to prepare themselves for a long-term relationship. In other words you are setting yourself up for a lot of heartache and grief. A relationship with two people who are adequately prepared is a lot of work. Can you imagine how much more difficult it is if neither one of you are prepared? Now that you have pondered that thought, think of how much more difficult it would be for you emotionally if you are prepared and the person you are involved with is still relationally immature.

Some will say *"How do you know that you will not be the one who will change their mind?"* My response to that question is quite simply *"How much time would you be willing to invest in waiting to find out?"* Those questions are subjective, based solely on you the individual. Do not let anyone tell you specifically how long you should wait, or what your boundaries are. That is based on what you know about yourself. If you are impatient and know that you do not want to wait long, be honest with yourself. To place yourself in the timeframe of a patient person will only increase your frustration level. However, this does not absolve you of the responsibility of working on your character flaws. You still must work on becoming the best possible you, so you can present yourselves to potential suitors. It begins with you knowing where you are in the process.

John Maxwell a popular motivational speaker stated in his Law of the Scoreboard that a team can only make adjustments when it knows where it stand. While ordinarily you may not consider yourself a team, you are a spirit, which has a soul, and you live in a body; and it is only as long as all three parts of you (spirit, mind, body) are in one accord can you maintain peace. Once one of those parts gets off course however, confusion will set in and that is when all hell can and will break loose in your life - literally. So one of the first steps in this process would be to honestly assess who you are. This cannot occur until you realize that the enemy is fighting against just that. He certainly does not want you to come into realization or how you are. In this area he steals, kills and destroys the truth of your identity long before you are aware that you have one.

Wisdom Key

"The enemy has skillfully eroded the family structure in our society, and as a result erased God's original intent from society."

Chapter 5

The Enemy's Attack Against Relationships

Contrary to what many would believe, the problem with broken relationships did not begin with the last few generations. This has been a problem which has been occurring since the Fall in the Garden, and we can see that the enemy has been busy since then. God instituted the family as the foundation of civilization, and what we are now living through in society today is the direct result of its breakdown.

I can recall one of my favorite movies the *Terminator*. In that movie the machines could not defeat John Carter in his time for during his era he was a strong leader. He had gathered the people with one purpose, and he was not only passing that information on to the current generation but, they were also training the younger generations. He was so successful that the machines were losing the battle. The machines decided to send a Terminator into the leader's past to destroy his mother before his birth. In the second movie the Terminator was sent to destroy the young leader before he realized who he was, and in the third movie before He stepped into his purpose. Well to make a long story short, I cannot help but see the similarities when we look at the war we have with the enemy. The bible tells us in John 12:31 that this war is already completed and that Satan's end is already determined. However, the enemy has no intention of going to his future alone. He plans to take as many of us human souls with him when he suffers his punishment. Using the same strategy as laid out in the Terminator movie, the enemy has focused on taking out the parents long before their children are born; and when that fails, taking out the children before they come into realization of who they are.

There is no denying that strong individuals are needed for strong families, and strong families are needed for strong communities. God was the one who ordained the family as the foundation and building block of the community, and this is what Satan has been working to erode since the Garden of Eden. While many would like to blame technological advancements such as social media, television, cell phones, etc. for the current plight of our society, that is incorrect. It is the breakdown of the family structure which has been having such a devastating effect on our society.

The family environment serves as the training center for

our children (of at least is should). Unfortunately, our embrace of the world's ways has led to the breakdown of our family structures, our values; and this is what has ultimately led to the breakdown of society. The enemy has skillfully eroded the family structure, and as a result erased God's original intent for society. Much like the Terminator who intended to wipe out John Carter before he even existed, the enemy seeks to erase the impact of a godly foundation upon your life, which will continue to have an impact on your offspring for years to come.

We all know that life is not like a movie and we cannot go back into our past to change our futures. In addition, unlike the movie life does not occur in 90 -120 minutes and does not always have a happy ending either. What we can take from this movie however, is that in order to wipe out the effects of the enemy, we can use the enemy's scheme against him and reconnect the individual to God's original intention for the family. That way, we can take our rightful place as leaders in the family's training facility to create strong individuals.

John Maxwell also refers to the family as a team: a group of people that interact together in business, ministry, sports, volunteer organizations, and family settings. In his popular book *The 17 Indisputable Laws of Teamwork*, he has identified one the 17 laws as the "law of the weakest link". In this law he states that a team can only grow as strong as its weakest link. Children have over the generations become violent, rebellious, and disrespectful. While we would like to view children as being the weakest link, they are not. The blame has be placed on the true culprit - it is our own *stinking thinking*, for we have accepted the world's way of thinking in everything including our dating experiences.

There are three things which has had a negative impact on the family: 1) working mothers; 2) absent fathers; and 3) same sex marriages. Whereas we once saw them as social problems, the sad reality is that it is now becoming the new norm, and the number of children growing up in these alternative households being raised with these skewed mindsets are also increasing. To make any headway in this area we must remember how God created the family to function and return to that foundation.

In summary, we must not forget that the enemy has been targeting families since the Garden of Eden. Just take a look at Adam and Eve's offspring! Cain killed his own brother Abel, and this trend is continuing. Sadly, this trend has not been limited to siblings either; as we often hear of children who are killing their parents simply because they want their inheritance or because they wouldn't let them do what they wanted to do. Where is this coming from? This is coming from the influence that the enemy has had on society. As society as a whole has chosen to deviate from God's plan, society as a whole is we are now reaping the results of that decision. Satan has been doing this for a long time, and he is also very good at it. We must understand that strong families are what lead to strong communities; and we must now impact future generations by returning to God's original plan.

Wisdom Key

*"Children must also learn that there are consequences to
every decision that they make, and some decisions have
lifelong and sometimes deadly consequences when we
consider the impact AIDS has had on mankind."*

Chapter 6

A Skewed Mindset

The educational environment was developed to teach and train our children according to God's principles; unfortunately, it is currently not functioning in that capacity. Having deviated from its foundational guidelines to teach individuals how to read so that they can study the bible for themselves, unfortunately the educational system is now contributing to the problem. The school environment has now become a place where our children are exposed to much more due to time, proximity, and now its teachings. For at least six hours a day children are exposed to the skewed ideologies offered by society through their peers and the curriculum.

Sex education teaches our children that same-sex marriages are okay and that passing out condoms is the answer to the problem of AIDS and teenage pregnancies.

Gone are the days where children were educated by the parents within the home, and because of the ease of transportation they are no longer sheltered from the immoral mindsets of societal deviants either. The school environment has now become the place where we breed them as they learn from their peers and teachers. The solutions offered are just mere band-aids which mask the problem, and does nothing to address the root problem.

Children need to learn more than how to protect themselves from sexual diseases, or to be tolerate of a situation which God has clearly stated to be an abomination. While we are not to hate the sinner, we must not turn a blind eye to the situation. Our children must first learn that sex is to be reserved for a close and intimate relationship with another individual. They must also learn that it is not okay to have sex outside the confines of that relationship, and it should be reserved for the sanctity of marriage. With that being said however, we must also operate in wisdom and realize that they are children and are apt to make mistakes. Some of them are going to give into the pressure from society and this is where the family and the church comes in. If the parents and the churches are functioning in the manner which God intended, parents would have already prepared their children long before the school has had the opportunity to influence them negatively. While this does not mean that they will not fall prey, they will at least have been given a chance.

This is what I refer to as the "Law of Whose First" - that which is first taught is the one thing which must be addressed to change their mindset. For example, a child that learns that it is wrong to steal within the home before they enter the school environment, when approached from their peers to steal their conscious kicks in to remind them that this is wrong. However, in the event that they do not receive this teachings prior to being approached, they are left without any safeguards in order to avoid that temptation. While relying on this alone is not enough to guarantee that they do not engage in this deviant behavior, it is necessary to understand how this principle works. Without this understanding, we as parents are responsible for the deviancy of our own children. We must teach them and reinforce the truth, and in the case of those more difficult (i.e. rebellious) use disciplinary actions. Children must also learn that there are consequences to every decision that they make, and some decisions have lifelong and sometimes deadly consequences. When we consider the impact AIDS has had on mankind, no one is exempt from the consequences - believers and non-believers suffer alike.

Abortion is another situation of dire concern. Individuals have learned that instead of enduring the consequences of their poor decision making they can "fix it" by getting rid of it. This mindset is implanted long before the act has occurred. The ideology that "if I get pregnant I can have an abortion" presents abortion as an option and method for birth control. This is not the message that we want our children to receive for they are not learning from their mistakes. In addition, through this action they demonstrate once again that they have a poor understanding of who God is. If they understand God to be the one who is the creator and the giver of life, they will recognize that God is the one who placed that baby within that mother's womb for procreation. That child is NOT a mistake and certainly NOT an accident!

Looking at the definition of accident, we see that it is defined by the Merriam-Webster's dictionary as follows:

a : an unforeseen and unplanned event or circumstance
b : lack of intention or necessity : chance <met by accident rather than by design>
2 a : an unfortunate event resulting especially from carelessness or ignorance
b : an unexpected and medically important bodily event especially when injurious <a cerebrovascular accident>
c : an unexpected happening causing loss or injury which is not due to any fault or misconduct on the part of the person injured but for which legal relief may be sought
d —used euphemistically to refer to an involuntary act or instance of urination or defecation (Merriam-Webster's Online Dictionary)

BREAKING THROUGH THE BARRIERS

Terms such as "unforeseen , unplanned, lack of intention, unfortunate, unexpected, involuntary, and nonessential indicate a situation out of one's control. Given that we know that procreation occurs out of the sexual experience, then people are very much in control of the outcome and cannot use the excuse that it was an accident. Given the alarming rate of unwanted pregnancies, we can only surmise that people truly believe that they can defy the laws of nature and engage in sexual activity without considering the consequences of their actions. This line of thinking is a clear indication of one's immaturity as many are still unwilling to assume responsibility for their actions. That in itself speaks for itself and warrants further discussion.

Section 3

Christian Dating:

Things You Need To Know

Wisdom Key

"We know that one of the most important factors on who has the influence on a young child is their mentors."

Chapter 7

The Necessity of Wise Counsel

Christian dating cannot occur if one does not have Christian teaching. Therefore, Christians adults, parents, caregivers, and leaders are essential in God's plan for future generations.

> *Hear, O Israel: The LORD our God, the LORD is one.*[a] *5 Love the LORD your God with all your heart and with all your soul and with all your strength. 6 These commandments that I give you today are to be on your hearts. 7 Impress them on your children. Talk about them when you sit at home and when you walk along the road, when you lie down and when you get up. 8 Tie them as symbols on your hands and bind them on your foreheads. 9 Write them on the doorframes of your houses and on your gates. Deuteronomy 6:4-9*

We know that one of the most important factors on who has the influence on a young child is their mentors. While the educational environment fulfills a great impact on our children, that was not God's original intent. Consider the following verses regarding role of mentors:

Train up a child in the way he should go; even when he is old he will not depart from it. Proverbs 22:6

Do not withhold discipline from a child; if you strike him with a rod, he will not die. If you strike him with the rod, you will save his soul from Sheol. Proverbs 23:13-14

Fathers, do not provoke your children to anger, but bring them up in the discipline and instruction of the Lord. Ephesians 6:4

Whoever spares the rod hates his son, but he who loves him is diligent to discipline him. Proverbs 13:24

The rod and reproof give wisdom, but a child left to himself brings shame to his mother. Proverbs 29:15

Folly is bound up in the heart of a child, but the rod of discipline drives it far from him. Proverbs 22:15

And if it is evil in your eyes to serve the Lord, choose this day whom you will serve, whether the gods your fathers served in the region beyond the River, or the gods of the Amorites in whose land you dwell. But as for me and my house, we will serve the Lord." Joshua 24:15

My son, keep your father's commandment, and forsake not your mother's teaching. Bind them on your heart always; tie them around your neck. Proverbs 6:20-21

You shall teach them diligently to your children, and shall talk of them when you sit in your house, and when you walk by the *way, and when you lie down, and when you rise. Deuteronomy 6:7*

Fathers, do not provoke your children, lest they become

discouraged. Colossians 3:2

These scriptures not only indicate the importance on preparation, but He also gives us specific guidelines on how to train the next generation. When we consider these scriptures, we must recognize the importance that God places on this assignment.

It is a sad evidence of the breakdown of our society's values when we hear of schools passing out condoms. This is certainly not what our forefathers intended when they developed our education system.

Daniel Webster as a leading American statesman and senator from Massachusetts during the period leading up to the Civil War. He argued a case involving the Philadelphia Public School which forbade ministers from being on campus, arguing before the court for 3 days on the importance of allowing religious instruction within the schools. The last day his argument was taken completely from the bible, and was built upon the following scripture taken from Mark 10:14:

> *Suffer the little children to come unto me and forbid them not, for of such is the kingdom of God (KJV)*

His argument was so effective that it was also published. The Supreme Court ruled in his favor and reversed the decision, supporting the belief that when the school encourages religious instruction or cooperates with religious authorities *they are following the best of traditions.* (Barton, 2004).

Benjamin Franklin who is also perceived as one of the least religious of our founding founders, was involved in the reprinting of the New England Primer which was the first textbook ever printed in America, and all students learned to read from it. This book had three core elements based on biblical scriptures and beliefs: the rhyming alphabet, alphabet of lessons for youth and a shorter Catechism for a beginning readers teaching the ten commandments. In his proposals related to the education of youth in Pennsylvania, the scope and content of the history class was to instruct in the advantage of a religious character among private person and the excellence of the Christian religion". Thomas Paine who was considered even less religious than Franklin, outspoke against schools which taught science without the influence of our "divine origin", stating that they were creating a generation of atheism which disregarded the influence of our creator. Our children are now learning about sex education in their health classes which include teaching about birth control and abortion, and yet abstinence is not even offered as an alternative; and it is associated more with personal pleasure that it is for procreation and for shared love and intimacy.

There is nothing saying that children should not learn about sex, in fact they should. However, it should be taught about in the confines of God's biblical standards. With a skewed ideology of what love is, and a lack of understanding about God's intention for sexual interaction, our children are bound to make the disastrous mistakes that they are making now when choosing a mate. So what are we doing to make sure that our children are receiving the right messages? We will now explore this question further in the next chapter.

Wisdom Key

" Children are our divine assignment from God. It is not enough that all of their basic needs are taken care of their needs. We must realize also that there is a difference between raising children and taking care of their needs. "

Chapter 8

A Parent's Responsibility

As I stated previously, there are three influences which have attributed to the breakdown of the family - working mothers, absent fathers, and same sex marriages. We will now explore these areas further.

For whatever reason it is, whether it is for the increased cost of living, or for the attainment of material wealth or status, it has became necessary for mothers to leave the household and enter the workforce. Data from the U.S. Bureau of Labor Statistics has shown that working mothers with children under the age of three rose by almost 10% in the 1990's, and by 2011 it was reported that 70.6% of mothers with children under the age of 18 was either employed or looking for work. They also report that mothers with children under the school age are at 63.9%. What is most alarming is that mothers with children under the age of one year are working at 55.8%.

Research reported that women with younger children are more likely to stay at home with their children; however, given the high teenage pregnancy rates and lower socioeconomic status, it is highly unlikely that the parent will possess the necessary skills to be successful in training their children. Also, with the additional concerns attributed to the increase of teenage pregnancies, divorce, and same sex marriages, the other influence has been removed from the household. Mothers who once attended to and provided the basic needs of the children in the household, are now no longer available to their children emotionally, mentally or physically; and by relying on outside agencies to take on the role of parents in our children's lives, we have allowed the world to have more impact on our children then ourselves.

The only way to reverse this negative trend is to return to biblical principles of parenting, and to take more seriously our role of parenting. Now what does this have to do with dating you ask? In light of this information, it is important that individuals who are dating place more emphasis on the long-term effects of their decisions, and while feelings are an important part of the process, our relationships should not be based upon them alone. As dating is the system in which we have accepted as our means to meet a qualified individuals to marry, this is where we must begin.

In order to develop a game plan to defeat the enemy, we must first understand that if he can get you to marry the wrong individual, he can ruin your life for decades and the lives of your offspring for generations to come. While we often do not think about this when we are dating, you must not forget that the decisions that you make now will have long-term consequences. Therefore, there are a few things that you must do to prepare for yourself beginning with how we view the dating relationship. First, parents must understand the importance God places on them assuming their responsibility for their children.

Children are a heritage from the LORD, *offspring a reward from him. Psalms 127:5*

Children are our divine assignment from God. It is not enough that all of their basic needs are taken care of. We must realize also that there is a difference between raising children and taking care of their needs.

Children need to learn from their parents; and parents need the experience of learning from their children. Parents can impart wisdom based upon their past personal experiences, and children can impart knowledge of their experiences in the present. That relationship is much like a choir singing a song together, each section, singing their own harmonious part, and yet at the same time they are coming together as one. Whether it is discipline, adolescence issues

71

or peer problems, time is needed to share a parent's wisdom, ethical and moral values as well as their personal convictions. This is important because the family is the first line of defense against negative peer pressure, and the ideals of our ever changing society.

In a study conducted in 1930 (Osburn), it was reported that the dilemma of the modern family was due to its loss of functions. He listed the functions as follows:

Economic – the family once was self-sufficient and produced and consumed what they needed; however since that is no longer the case, banks, stores and factories are now needed.

Family gave prestige and status – a member of a family was less of an individual and more of a member of a family; whereas they were more concerned at how the family was impacted by their actions and behaviors

Education – was completed in the home, but children were also taught vocations at home

Protection – the father provided protection for children, but children paid back by providing economic and psychological needs of parents in their old age

Religious – grace, family prayers, and reading of the Bible together
Recreation – n
ow done at recreation centers outside of the home, school, community, or health clubs.

Affection – between mates and also the procreation of children.

A new generation of children emerged in the 70's when parents found that they were not able to afford the cost of childcare. These children have been identified as latch key children, in other words those children left with no adult supervision. The result was a group of children with little or no parental guidance or interaction in their lives. Because children need to be guided, directed and steered in the right direction, the result is a group of children who lack a respect of authority. The sad reality is that families are spending less and less time together, and are learning less and less about God's ideal plan.

Christian households are taught in Prov. 29:15 that *"The rod and reproof give wisdom: but a child left [to himself] bringeth his mother to shame."* Without guidance and direction, children will ultimately bring shame to their parent(s) by being rebellious and defiant. This has unfortunately resulted in a new breed of individuals who do not respect the authority figures in their lives (parents, teachers, police, etc...) – we call them *juvenile delinquents*. And once again unfortunately, outside agencies are becoming better equipped to handle these children as well in foster care, group homes, and youth detention facilities. The result is a group of children, who lacking parental guidance are growing up with no one to discipline them, and no one to teach the importance of respecting authority. This group of people who ultimately feel as if they do not fit in, eventually gravitate to a group of individuals who are just like them. Everyone needs to feel as if they belong somewhere, and unfortunately many youth (and some adults) find it with the social misfits of society. Until we place our priorities back where they belong in the proper training of our children; the result will be a society raising up and sending out a generation of children who are lost, disillusioned and ill-equipped to handle the pressures of living up to and reaching their full potential in life.

Wisdom Key

"The only way to develop healthy relationships in our present is to be honest about our relationships in the past."

Chapter 9

Individual Responsibility

Churches spend a lot of time teaching women how to live their lives according to Proverbs 31; however, there is very little information offered on what kind of man who is equipped to handle the Proverbs 31 women. This is important because Christians are not receiving the information they need to ensure that they have successful relationships. Believing that the church is the place to teach us how to live life on this earth, additional resources are necessary to provide this guidance. Reflecting upon my dating experiences, I realize that I just like everyone else, had a lot of misconceptions.

There are a lot of books out there on how to date, the importance of healthy relationships, but information created specifically for Christians continue to offer vague information. This places Christians at a serious disadvantage

as they fail to learn how to prepare for the most important
relationship in their life - marriage.   This is most unfortunate
for singles in the 21st century, who are left to fend for
themselves as caregivers are no longer responsible to find
them suitable mates. This means that as we leave our parent's
household and assume responsibility for our own lives, we
are also responsible for finding our own mates. While the
world has changed, God never intended for women to step
out from under their covering. Left without any instructions
on how to find their mates, Christians have had to rely on the
world's way of doing things, and this has had a negative long-
term impact on Christian families.

A commonly accepted misconception is that women are
emotional beings. While there may be a great deal of women
who are, there are still many more who are just not in touch
with their feelings. This is just as true for men. Whatever the
case may be, we must remember that we were all created with
emotions, and we were created by God that way. Men are
prone to and experience emotions just like women do, and
although many would like to believe not as often as women,
that is simply not the case, and our past relationships can be
the key to our future ones.

Our emotions are there to help us, that is if we let them.
With that being said, we must also be aware that they can also
hinder us if we are not in tune with them. I heard someone

say that they had an amicable breakup. Well what in the world does that mean? When a relationship ends there is a lot of emotional pain, especially if you are truly in love. I am more inclined to believe that all relationships that end are ending badly. If things were great - you would not be breaking up. Someone is going to be hurt! The pain is the result of the conflict, and out of adversity can be birthed emotional pain or great love. Unfortunately, many of us choose the former and the result is a life of discouragement, frustration and self-sabotage as we continue to set ourselves up to be hurt. The worst thing about self-sabotage is that we are not aware that our relationships are failing because of our own insecurities and low self-esteem. If you do not believe that you are worthy of the best, you will always question the intentions of others. This is what I refer to as the foggy lens. Much like the obscured view of a pair of glasses which are dirty, we begin to view the people in our lives based on a faulty mindset. The only way to develop healthy relationships in our present is to be honest about our relationships in the past. There is truth to the ideology that we can be our own worst enemy. If we are not true to ourselves, it is impossible to be true to others, and we are only deceiving ourselves.

Now let us keep in mind that not all emotions are not bad. Healthy emotions can help us to intuitively know things, to be understanding and empathetic, to communicate with others, and also to protect us in the presence of danger. This will ultimately prepare us to be better parents, friends, and individuals. However, given that emotions are fickle and can change from moment to moment, any decision that results in lifelong consequences should never be made based upon them alone. Yet, that is exactly what many of us are willing to do when we place more importance on how we feel about an individual, and how they feel about us in a dating relationship. Marriage is one the many important decisions that we make in our lifetimes. Asking someone the question "Do you love them?" is just not enough. Some practical, common sense will make the world of difference in this process.

The bible tells us in Proverbs 11:14 that there is safety in the multitude of counsel, and in the dating stage of development that safety can save one from a lot of heartache later on in life. Proverbs 15:22 goes so far to tells us that plans actually fail without advisors.

Plans fail for lack of counsel, but with many advisers they succeed. Many of our relationships are destined for failure as we have not even taken the time to establish a plan beforehand. Before embarking on this journey, you must first 1) know yourself; 2) know how to recognize a potentially good mate, and finally 3) how to maintain a healthy relationship. This section will focus on you determining who you are, for you are the qualifying factor in all of your relationships. You must begin with asking yourself the right questions.

Before we can even address how to identify the right type of mate, you have to first ask yourself "Why is it that I think I am ready for marriage?" If you do not have an answer to that question, then please save the rest of the dating world from the pleasure of your company. Remain content at staying at the friendship stage and save someone else from some much unwanted heartache and grief. This stage is only for those who have spent time contemplating a lot more on what they have to bring to a relationship, and a lot less time on what it is that they want from it. While knowing what it is that you want is important, it is not as important as ensuring that you are ready and have something to bring into the table.

So what makes a good mate? Some would say someone who is conscientious, responsible, a good problem-solver, possess good conflict resolution skills, kind etc... Sounds like a job description doesn't it? Dating can be viewed much like a job interview. Before presenting yourself for consideration, make sure that you are qualified! While we can still learn from our mistakes, in this particular situation you are not alone. In this method of learning you are also risking the emotional health of another human being, and if you don't care - then that is yet another reason why you do not need to be dating.

Other things to prepare for include financial, mental, and emotional health. If you are not taking care of yourself physically, have poor money management skills, are emotional, and have poor mental health just to name a few, I would say give yourself a little more time to get in control of yourself so that you can have something to offer in the relationship. I also encourage you to look for these same characteristics in the individual that you are considering as a potential mate. I caution you however, that these should all be reviewed on an individual basis. A person who is in high debt as a result of student loans for a completed college degree, is a lot different than someone who has students loans on a degree they did not complete.

You must remember that in all of your relationships that you are presenting yourself as being ready. In a dating relationship, that means that you are presenting yourself as being marriage ready. Once you get married, things change considerably, "theirs' and "mine" becomes "ours". Additionally, it would be beneficial for you to consider physical health if you know that this is going to be a problem area for you. Although it may appear to others that you are being superficial, let me remind you that you are the one making a lifetime commitment. You are the one who will have to live with that individual, not the individual who has chosen to judge you; and you are going to have to live with your decision and not them. I also encourage you to take into consideration the feelings of your potential mate, and how they would feel years later if you were to end the relationship as a result of their physical ailments. Save them and yourself a lot of avoidable frustration by carefully considering these areas beforehand. The point of this section is to make sure that you not only know what you want out of the relationship, but you are to be absolutely sure that you are ready for a relationship. Your purpose should be to add to someone else's happiness and not to subtract from it. Now make sure you understand clearly here that it is not your job to make someone else happy. That is their job! If they are not happy by themselves guess what, they are definitely NOT going to be happy with you. There is a great deal of truth to the cliche "misery loves company". There is nothing more discouraging then to find out later on that you have invested a great deal of time and energy into the life of someone who really had nothing to offer. Make sure that you are not that person. Take the time to prepare yourself, and you can enter the dating world qualified and equipped to be successful.

Wisdom Key

"There are several areas that the church does not want to address, and it just so happens that dating is one of them."

Chapter 10

The Responsibility of the Church

For far too long congregations have been sitting by and allowing the local Church to teach our children about the things of God. Many of the problems in society today are because we just did not know what to pour into our children. However, as we consider and ponder the habits and examples provided to us since the beginning of time, we will find that it was always God's intentions that the parents assume that responsibility. The problem is that we have many generations who had not have the privilege of being schooled by their parents. As a result, the church has had no choice but to pick up the slack in that area; however, the church has not made any progress in that area because either they are not aware that they have that responsibility, or (2) they themselves do not know what they should be teaching. So how do we remedy this situation?

The answer lies in knowledge. It is important that the church receive the information that they need in this area so that they can pour this information into the body of Christ, who will in turn take this information and pour it into the current and the next generation. Therefore, it is essential that the church focus on what they should be teaching. I would say that it is essential that the church teaches everything that I had discussed previously. There are several areas that the church fails to or does not want to address and it just so happens that dating is one of them.

Youth and children need to know that dating has a divine purpose and it is not just so that they can have fun and sex. Is that too harsh for you? Well this is the kind of world that we live in, and this is how we need to speak to our youth and young adults. We have to be straightforward and speak honestly about the truth, and the truth is that God does not smile on fornication. For those of you who need a more direct explanation, that would be sex before marriage. God feels so strongly about it that it is mentioned in the bible. I Cor. 6:18 it says:

> *Flee from* **sexual immorality.** *Every other sin a person commits is outside the body, but the sexually immoral person sins against his own body. 1 Cor. 6:18 (ESV).*

Let's take a look at Galatians 5:19-21. It says here that

these people will not inherit the kingdom of God.

> *Now the works of the flesh are evident: sexual immorality, impurity, sensuality, idolatry, sorcery, enmity, strife, jealousy, fits of anger, rivalries, dissensions, divisions, envy, drunkenness, orgies, and things like these. I warn you, as I warned you before, that those who do such things will not inherit the kingdom of God.*

Now that we know that sex before marriage is wrong, we also have to take into consideration other kinds of relationships which God frowns upon as well which includes anything which will "defile the marriage bed".

> *marriage be held in honor among all, and let the marriage bed be undefiled, for God will judge the sexually immoral and adulterous. Heb. 13:4 (ESV).*

What does it mean to defile the marriage bed? While many of us would not deliberately do anything which would be considered defilement to their marriage bed; however, we must also be careful that we do not do it unintentionally. Coming from a place where I once believed that it was okay to indulge in my sexual fantasies, I must be careful that I do not compare my future mate (or spouse) to my previous sexual exploits.

For example, if I am with my husband and thinking about a previous sexual encounter, I am in fact defiling my marriage bed, for it is not fair to my husband to be compared with previous relationships. Defilement also includes other things such as pornography, homosexuality and bestiality. However, if you have done this in the past, do not worry for all is not lost. Our God is a good and merciful God, and once we repent and turn from our wicked ways, He is faithful to forgive us. The keys terms to remember here are *repent and turn from*. Many saints incorrectly believe the confessing of sins before God and asking for forgiveness is repentance. Well, it is not! True repentance does involve those steps but, you also are required to take it a step further. True repentance requires a turning away from that sin as well. We must turn our backs on anything which is ungodly and actions in our lives which would grieve the Holy Spirit. Now before we go any further we must address the issue of homosexuality.

This is a touchy area in the body of Christ. In light of *gay pride* and *LGET* departments popping up everywhere, the church has let down their guard in this area. Don't get me wrong we just respect these individuals are they are loved by God just like we are; however, we must be careful that we do not condone this and allow them to pour this ideology into our children's mindsets. In addition, because people who are in the church open themselves up to receive the spiritual influence of the individual who is leading, we must be careful to remain alert and to pay attention to the spirits of our leaders. So what does that mean? Let's explore this further.

Homosexuality, bestiality, pornography, etc. all derive from the influence of a spirit of lust. Contrary to what many would believe it is not only limited to sins of a sexual nature. A spirit of lust is the culprit when you allow anything to stop you from fulfilling the will of God. You are in the case seeking to fulfill your own desires instead of God's desire for your life. Now that we have cleared that up, let's focus specifically on the sins of a sexual nature - fornication, adultery, and any sexual perversions.

Fornication as mentioned previously as something that God does not want us to do. Contrary to what many would lead you to believe, God is not trying to take the fun out of your life. In fact it is the exact opposite, He is trying to protect you. There are many negative emotions associated with previous sexual relationships, especially if the individual chooses not to marry you, and it can be more detrimental to a woman than it is to a man.

Through the process of sexual relations is how a women's soul is bound to her mate. As our soul consists of our mind, will, intellect, and our emotions. While I am not saying that men are not impacted emotionally (because they are), as women are prone to be more emotional than men; and this is also another discussion which it outside the confines of this book. However, can you now see why it could potentially be more of a concern with women than with men? Essentially, sexual promiscuity creates a soul tie with every individual that one has slept with, and this soul tie is the reason why many continue to physically long for their sexual partner long after the relationship has ended. I personally believe that although it is not specifically identified in the bible, that this is the reason why many end up in the repetitive cycle of ending up with the same kind of individual over and over again. This is what they long for, and we as humans are always moving toward that which is comfortable for us and brings pleasure, we are often drawn to that which we desire or brings us pleasure.

In a nutshell to break the negative cycle which is perpetuating itself in society, the body of Christ must return to the basics. We must live our lives as an example and model godly principles, which will in turn positively influence society to turn from their wicked ways. That may mean approaching a very difficult subject. The church must be willing to fill in the gaps where parents are failing, the church must be willing to talk about sex.

Section 4
Christian Dating:

Principles to Guide You

Wisdom Key

"Remember, you are created in God's image, and anything created in his image is precious. You are a magnificent treasure, a rare diamond indeed, and there is a mate for you just as magnificent, rare, and precious.

Chapter 11

Dating Rules

There are some keys things that one must take into consideration when looking for that perfect mate, and I refer to them as dating rules. While I do not propose that you will not make any mistakes if you follow them, I will state that you will have a better chance at finding a godly and morally sound mate if you use them as a guideline.

1.   *Understand the principle of being" evenly yoked"!*

We already discussed the reason why we are not be unevenly yoked spiritually however, unevenly yoked is not only limited to salvation. Unevenly yoked can also be applied to areas such as spiritual beliefs, education, politics, how to raise children, are a few areas to mention. While in some areas there should be clear guidelines set, in other areas there could be some leeway, and you just "agree to disagree" and move beyond that. In any event, one should have established those areas long before they decide to begin dating, and then communicated to your potential mate long before a serious commitment is made. Many of problems that people have in marriage are those things that they did not take the time to discuss prior to the "I do!" Do not negate the importance of knowing who you are, and to establish what you will or will not tolerate before you start presenting yourself to another for consideration.

So how do you discover who you are? It starts with knowing what your likes and dislikes are. Did you know that two people can be unevenly yoked in the way they communicate? While this is something that cannot be addressed directly as communication styles can change, it is something that you have to be aware of before you get involved in a tumultuous relationship. For example if I know that I am an individual who enjoys healthy debates and discussions, while I may be embarking on what I would view as a healthy discussion, if my potential mate negatively views confrontation or does not know how to verbally engage themselves, to them I may appear as being argumentative. Can you see how this can quickly become a volatile situation? There is nothing saying that these two cannot get along, but it is certainly going to require some understanding. At least if you are aware of your differences, you have positioned yourself to be able to adapt, or to least find some alternative avenues to satisfy your needs. This is however impossible to accomplish if you do not understand yourself. or do not know how to communicate your needs to your potential mate. Until then, if you are expecting someone else to understand you by "reading between the lines" you are in for a rude awakening. This is no different than expecting others to read your mind, and as we all know this is clearly impossible for anyone to do.

In the case that one is unable to communicate verbally, there is nothing saying that you cannot resort to other forms of communication such as writing letters or notes. What I am saying however, if you do not establish a way of communicating with one another there may be dire consequences. This is a self-sabotaging behavior in which you are the one who is not allowing another individual the opportunity to get to know you, and ultimately rob yourself of any chance of intimacy in your life.

2.   *Do not assume that age equates with maturity!*

A mature individual is one who can express their thoughts, feelings and ideas. While not everyone is perfect in that area, beware of the deer in the headlights syndrome. If you do this several times and the reaction is the same, chances are you are dealing with someone who has a problem with communication. It does not mean that they don't care, it may only mean that they don't know how to express it. If combined with other warning signs however, it may mean exactly that.

Let's be honest, one's biological age is not an indicator of maturity. A young child has to learn how to change their clothes, pick up behind themselves, learn how to control their temper, and eventually learn to live by themselves to grow up to be responsible adults. The harsh reality is that there are people who never learned to grow up and still very much rely on their parents for many things. Whether you are a man or woman makes no difference, there is no room in your life for a potential mate if that office is still held by a parent or anyone else. Before you can bring someone else into your life, that office must be vacant and you must be responsible for yourself. If you doubt the validity of this, talk to a woman who has dated a "mama's boy" or a man who has dated "daddy's little girl". There is nothing more discouraging to a potential mate to see that someone else is more important to them outside of God.

The bible says that a man is to leave and cleave to his wife, and a wife is to leave her daddy's home to now rely on her husband. If you believe that you are going to change their mind do not waste your time, and if you are the culprit it is time that you grow up. If you don't, you are placing your potential mate at a considerable disservice, especially if you are dividing your time between the two of them. The office of partner is to held by your mate, and not shared between mate and parent. If you are not ready for that yet, at least take into consideration how you would feel if you always had to vie for the attention of your mate. If you are least honest, as a man you wouldn't like it if your wife did not trust you to take care of her needs or at least give you the chance to prove yourself; and a woman does not like it when a man's mother is more of priority than she is.

3. *Your Relationship Will Not Complete You, Only Enhance You!*

If you are looking for that someone to complete you - forget it! A relationship is not the place to look for your completeness but a place to share it. If you are not pouring into the life of that individual, you are essentially doing the opposite and draining from them. Entering a relationship with this mentality only sets up the person for failure as you should be as whole and as complete as you can possibly be before attempting to partner with another individual.

The reason that I say " as whole" and "as complete" is because some things will not be identified until you are in a relationship. In that case your mate will be in a position to help you to address those areas. To knowingly enter a relationship without addressing your incompleteness will countermine your chances for a successful relationship, and also sets the other individual up for emotional pain. This is because you have unrealistic expectations for the other person to live up to, and your deficits will place considerable drain on them emotionally. We all have the responsibility of catering to our own person first spiritually, emotionally, mentally, as well as physically.

Most of us have already heard that we are a spirit, we have a soul (mind, will & intellect) and we live in the body, but let me reiterate it. If we do not cater to each of these areas in our lives, we will eventually become unbalanced. If you don't believe me, see how long you will live if you decided to fast continually to feed your spirit and forget about your body. You will eventually die, and you won't be any further use to God, the church, or anyone else for that matter! It sounds crazy doesn't it? Think about it though, there are many people out there who are feeding their spirit-man and forgetting about the rest of those areas in their lives. They are emotionally unstable and draining the very life out of the very people who love them. They place very little emphasis of how I can add to the happiness on someone else, but more of what it is that I need to be happy.

To anyone who have been involved in a relationship like this before, you know exactly what I am talking about. You wake up one day to discover that your love tank is seriously depleted because you have given so much into the relationship and have received nothing in turn. Please note that there is nothing wrong with giving because the bible says that it is better to give than to receive, but if you find that you are the one who is always doing and giving and getting nothing in return, it is time to throw in the towel and walk away. While they may think they are respecting you because they are not trying to fornicate and they are saying the right things, they are not. For if they truly cared for you they would be willing to pour into you in any way that they knew how to meet your needs as well. In addition, they should respect you enough to tell you the truth. It is not honorable to keep this information to yourself. If you know that the person you are dating is marriage minded and considering you as a potential mate, you owe it to them to tell them the truth. If you are holding on them because you are benefitting from the relationship, well that speaks for itself for it is nothing less than selfishness, and far from being respectful.

4.   *Understand the importance of balance in the body, soul, and spirit.*

So once again I ask "What is a godly mate"? While one can have their heads so far into the clouds that they are looking for someone who has an intimate relationship with God, a note of caution must also be considered as everything may not always be as it appears. One must not assume that everyone who has an anointing has an intimate relationship with God. Let me explain myself fully here.

All three parts of the spirit, soul, and body must be addressed. While we want to get to the point where our individual godly spirits dictate the decisions we make for those other areas, we do not want to get to the point where we negate those other areas. For example, an individual (male or female) can spend all of their time catering to their spiritual man and forget that they also must address their emotional and mental well being as well. This individual while they may have an understanding of spiritual principles and concepts, often lack a true understanding of their purpose which is to live our lives in a manner which would draw others into the kingdom. Many people would find it difficult to trust the judgment of a Christian who lacks emotional and mental stability. Therefore, when looking for a mate who is worthy of what you have to offer, you must begin with someone who not only caters not to their spiritual man, but who attends to their physical, mental and emotional health as well. They must be a well rounded individuals or they will not know how to care for the gift that is being given to them.

5.   *Understand what it means to be a Proverbs 31 Mate (male or female)*

Jesus said that there is no greater love than to lay down your life for a friend. While many people will say that to you, very few people will be willing to do so. How many people could you honestly say that you would be willing to lay down your life for? Many parents could say yes for their children, but I submit that the number of people on that list would be very small. Jesus demonstrated the perfect example of perfect love by teaching us how to love even those who persecute us, which he modeled for us on the cross. God never intended for us to give up our lives like Jesus did, but so many women do it every day. They give up their own identity in order to become that perfect mate for a man, failing to realize their role in the man's life. You see is the one who takes a supportive role, and she provides the support that the man needs to become all that he can be.

All Christian women know about and try to model their lives after the Proverbs 31 woman; however many fail to consider that Proverbs 31 are words of wisdom given to King Lemuel from his mother. Instructions given in this chapter include not to give his strength to a woman or his wisdom to those who purpose is to destroy kings; to avoid drinking lest he forgets who he is and the law; and not to pervert justice due to the afflicted. Proverbs 31:10 even begins with "a capable, intelligent, and virtuous woman - who is he who can find her? This scripture is directed to the man not the woman. The rest of the chapter describes to the man what to look for in a woman. You see, it takes a special kind of man who is able to recognize the qualities of a good woman. In trying so hard to become the Proverbs 31 woman, many women actually forget to wait for the man who recognizes who she is.

A good woman is like a rare jewel which has to be discovered, and according to Proverbs 31:10 "she is far more precious than jewels and her value is far above rubies or pearls". How many men out there really know the value of a good women? Many of her treasures are buried deep within her, and do not become evident until she has a man with a vision to support. While some things will already be evident such as her willingness to work and productivity, until she has a mate to support she cannot obtain her full potential as a helpmate.

Men is it your job to recognize the potential in the woman. Much like diamonds which are produced in the earth and under pressure, so is the Proverbs 31 woman created. Give her a vision because a women who has a man with a vision is in her optimal environment. Why? Because her efforts when combined with yours help to propel you into your destiny as head of household. In other words, her purpose in that relationship is to work with you as a helpmate, so that you can fulfill your vision in your personal life, in the family, and in the kingdom.

So what happens when a women is partnered with a man who has no vision? While a woman does have her own individual assignment, that assignment is somehow tied to a higher purpose which is a combined assignment for both her and her husband together. Following the pattern established in the Garden of Eden, God gives the vision to the man and they (the man and the woman) work together as one to complete their combined assignment.

6. *Make sure that you are, and look for signs that they are in touch with their own emotions.*

A women's intuition is a gift which is not to be ignored but embraced. While she may not understand it herself at first, she will feel and sense things long before the man does, which will be optimal in helping her mate relationally. A women's intuition and a man's ingenuity are to work hand in hand in problem-solving and strategic planning throughout the marriage, for there is no room for independence when two are working on becoming as one. While I am not saying that men cannot be intuitive, and women cannot be ingenious, what is more important is that they work together.

Unknown to many there is a difference between independence and interdependence. Women who are independent feel that they have no need for a man and yet, they often find themselves longing for one. Could it be that love is just an innate desire to be reunited with the one she received her rib from? How else could we explain the desire to find a soul mate? It is important to realize that if happiness is not personally attained first, there is no way it will be found when you are combined with another individual. The answer lies in being true to yourself first. Once you are complete and whole which means one in your mind, spirit and body; you can then give yourself wholly and completely to live interdependently with another whole individual.

Notice that I stated *another whole individual*. Interdependence then is your ability to maintain your identity while using that identity to combine with another to work towards something even greater than yourself. In order words, a man and woman must work together to fulfill the God-ordained vision for their marriage, for that vision cannot be accomplished on their own. They are both important equals submitting their gifts, talents and abilities to complement one another. committed to completing their combined assignment. However in the process of becoming one, you must not forget that they are still an individual. Much like the second, minute and hour hands of a clock working simultaneously and dependant on each other, the marriage vision is no different with each stage of development dependent upon one another. You must first be confident in your own identity, then become competent in your identity with your spouse, and only then can two complement one another in fulfilling their assignment.

7.   *Invest the time to study one another.*

   I believe that we all have been guilty of this one,

especially if we have been alone for a long time. We have all heard the term *Falling in love at first sight*. Well that is just a mere moment of temporary insanity where one throws out all remnants of rationalization and logic. This can be equated to the same thing as jumping off a cliff, and hoping that there is a body of water down there to catch your falling carcass. Sounds illogical doesn't it? The same is true when you believe that the person that you just met is prepared for you. As I said previously, it requires commitment, time and much effort. You are increasing your chances of having a successful relationship if you invest the time needed to learn about the individual you are dating. However, be careful of the individual who takes too long to make a decision as there may be other issues to contend with. The important thing to remember is that it does require time to get to know another individual. Investing time in the beginning, will save you a lot of heartache and grief later.

Communication in its simplest form is to speak clearly so that the other person understands the message which is begin conveyed. This is impossible to accomplish if the people doing the communicating do not know or understand each other. This is because the way an individual interprets a message is based upon their individual experiences.

As head of household, it does not mean that the man rules in every area, for if he was strong in every area there would be no need for him to have a helpmate. As the wife submits to her husband in his area of strengths, he must also submit to her area of strengths. Much like a company which operates with a team of leaders, the household must be no different. As the husband operates as the team leader and visionary, his wife would serve as the second in command responsible for her areas; both of them working together to accomplish the same goal. This would however require them to be able to communicate with one another. Therefore, if you are dating someone that you cannot communicate with you are heading for disaster. There is no way that you can even work on the smaller issues such as the breakdown of household chores. Even though it may seem like a small issue when you are dating, keep in mind that this is one of the biggest issues after many years of marriage. It does not take long for something that begins as a molehill to quickly become a mountain because it was left unaddressed.

When giving seminars on communication, I often begin with the picture of the caveman who has found his mate and is dragging her by the hair into his cave. While many would find this picture barbaric and comical, this is often how many people communicate. One person has their mind made up about something, and yet as a result of not expressing it to the other individual they are left to be dragged along kicking and screaming without any clear understanding of where they are going or why. There is no doubt that you are communicating, however this is a clear example of failing to communicate well.

When you have successfully communicated with another, even if they do not agree at least if they understand it can possibly lessen any opposition. However, if you finding that there is considerable dissension perhaps you should explore whether you are communicating your thoughts clearly. Effectively communicating can make the world of difference in any relationship as it increases respect and understanding, and is not limited to dating.

Communication is more than just expressing your thoughts clearly, for it is a circular process involving expressing, listening. receiving and responding. It is a time of sharing where both parties must be willing to share of their themselves, and to listen to what the other person is sharing about themselves.

If a potential mate refuses to talk about their past history or previous relationships, this could spell "danger ahead". It may mean that they have something to hide or they have something that they do not want to face. One thing is for sure, there is a reason why the other relationships ended, and it is something you need to know. Take the time to ask about past relationships, and pay particular attention to how much they are willing to admit or disclose. Remember that there are always two sides to every story, and I assure you each party contributed somehow to the demise of the relationship. While I am not saying that some behavior patterns cannot be changed, what I am saying is that behavior patterns that one is not aware of will never be changed.

8.   *Make sure that they know, understand and demonstrate godly love.*

Many people are not capable of handling true love, for many people do not know how to love themselves. We each have the responsibility of loving ourselves first, and then to love our neighbors "as" ourselves. Without experiencing self-love there is nothing in which to measure this love by. This is an assignment that only a true man or woman of God is capable of handling, for one cannot appreciate their gift unless they appreciate and accept the love that God has given so freely to us.

There is a distinct difference between godly and humanly love. Godly love is unconditional and human love is conditional. We often hear of people falling in and out of love after a period of time. This is something which we find common in teenagers as they are immature and are still discovering themselves. However, it is also no longer common for a couple to maintain their marriage vows "until death does them part".

In an Marriage Study conducted in Oklahoma (2002) it was reported that while Christians had more of the qualities that a couple needed to avoid divorce, Professor Stanley and his team report that Christians do divorce. However, good news does come from this study "Whether young or old, male or female, low-income or not, those who said that they were more religious reported higher average levels of commitment to their partners, higher levels of marital satisfaction, less thinking and talking about divorce and lower levels of negative interaction. These patterns held true when controlling for such important variables as income, education, and age at first marriage."

Modeling godly love is the only way that a man can learn to love his wife as himself. Ephesians 5:25 states "husbands love your wives, as Christ loves the Church". Without that as a foundation, a man is unable to love his wife, and this is something that must be accomplished long before he attempts to bring his "rib" into his life. So women, the first thing you should ask herself before you choose to date a man is "Does he know and understand the love of God?" The answer to that question does not lie in what he says, but it lies in what he does.

So how does a man demonstrate that he knows how to love? While it is true that a man must be fruitful, productive, know how to subdue, and have dominion over his own life, for him to take on that responsibility for another's life he must also learn how to adjust to the delicacies of this godly creation. Not only must he understand the woman and who she is in the bundle of her emotions and idiosyncrasies, he must also understand and be in touch with his own emotions. A man who understands and knows how to express his emotions is in the perfect place to bond and connect with his soul mate. Until he is able to do so, he will only perceive his mate as being emotional and irrational; in fact, belittling the very things which make her who she is.

9. *Pay attention to how they handle conflict and anger.*

Pay attention to how s/he handles conflict. There is nothing more frustrating than being married to someone who lacks in this area. If the individual you are dating cannot handle conflict or confrontation, there will be many issues which will be left unresolved in your relationship. Try to imagine what life will be like after many days, weeks, months and years with an accumulation of unresolved issues. Speaking from the view of this woman, this can lead to a lot of anger, resentment, bitterness, and eventually I no longer felt safe in my relationship. I can only imagine how difficult this would be for a man as well. This is the reason that *good* communication is essential for a healthy relationship.

Sharing is another area of grave concern. It profits the relationship very little if one person is the one doing all of the sharing and the other is not; or if one person shares and the others fails to listen or to respond. A lack of response is generally perceived by another that they just do not care or are not interested. While that may not be true, if it is not communicated this can cause the one who is sharing to withdraw, and can also lead to further negative emotions such as frustration, resentment, anger and bitterness if this a continually practice over a period of time. For women, this can have serious consequences as it may cause her to feel as if her emotions are not safe, which can further hinder her ability to submit.

There are many fallacies when it comes to the area of submission; and sadly many relationships have ended or in trouble because they fail to understand this premise. Submission, often equated with obedience is incorrect, and anyone who believes that I respectfully submit that they are sadly mistaken.

Submission is defined as follows: 1) to yield to governance of authority, 2) to present or propose to another for review; 3) to permit oneself to be subjected to something, or 4) to defer to or consent to abide by the opinion of or authority of another (Merriam-Websters Dictionary, 2012). While I am not saying that biblical submission is the same as worldly submission, what I am saying is that they are similar in that its implies an action on the part of the one doing the submitting. They make a decision to *yield* themselves to another. With that being said submission is much like respect, if you have to ask for it then obviously you do not have it; and perhaps it is because the conditions for submission have not yet occurred. Women you are expected to respect your husband. If you do not respect the man you are dating - do not marry him, and the same goes for men. You are expected to love your wife as Christ loved the church. If you do not think that you can do that - then do not marry her!

10. Do not submit until they commit!

This step sounds a lot easier than it actually is, but before two can become one flesh, the woman and her husband must understand the meaning of true submission. Often when we hear of the word submission we think only of the woman, however the man and the woman must submit to one another (Eph 5:21 KJV). In another version (NLT) it says "And further, submit to one another out of reverence for Christ". That is the role of a wife but not until you become a wife.

It is a bad situation when you are committed to someone who is not committed to you. The frustration of sitting by the phone waiting for the phone to ring, or emails, texts, and messages going unanswered only increases as the days go by. While it is easier said than done, do not waste your time and energy on someone who is obviously not interested in you. You deserve better than that, and you deserve someone who is going to want you just as much as you want them. Remember, you are created in God's image, and anything created in his image is precious. You are a magnificent treasure, a rare diamond indeed, and there is a mate for you just as magnificent, rare, and precious.

Wisdom Key

"Just because someone holds a high ranking position in a ministry does not mean that they are spiritually mature; and on the same token, you cannot assume that just because someone demonstrates a spiritual maturity that they can handle relationships."

Chapter 12

Dangers of Choosing the Wrong Mate

In a previous chapter I stated that "not everything that looks good is good", and there is definitely some truth to that statement. Just because someone holds a high ranking position in a ministry does not mean that they are spiritually mature; and on the same token, you cannot assume that just because someone demonstrates a spiritual maturity that they can handle relationships. I have made the mistake of assuming that someone in a spiritual position of authority and respected by many would make a good partner for me . Well I could not be further from the truth. It did not take long for me to realize that holding a spiritual position of authority does not equate to spiritual maturity, and having spiritual maturity does not equate to relationship maturity. The purpose of this chapter is to alert you to the dangers of marrying the wrong individual, and this is a section which should not be taken lightly.

We hear people talking about all the time about the benefits of being married, the blessing in finding one's soul mate, that perfect individual who will complete you. Why? Because everyone wants to be in love and live happily ever after. There is one thing that we should add to that discussion, the dangers of marrying the wrong individual. So the question remains who is the wrong individual?

You can get yourself together financially, deal with all of past hurts, fixed all of the problems that you had in your previous relationships but, there is one thing that you cannot do, and that is know the heart of another individual. Even if you have all the right rules, and do all of the right things, you must remember that there are some things that only God knows. Getting final approval from the Holy Spirit is the final step in this process.

As I look back over my previous relationships, I realize that there were some definite signs which were clearly misinterpreted or ignored by me; however, there were also some other things which would never have manifested themselves until the right situation presented itself. For example, for a crop to grow successfully the right conditions must exist - the right soil, with the right nutrients, and the right amount of water. Well the same is true for a relationship,. Remember, that which is hidden will eventually come to light; however, that may not occur until the right conditions present themselves.

There are several other instances which I could share but, I have chosen not to for obvious reasons. After many occurrences of having to defend myself of things of which I was not doing, the day came that I realized that the person I was dating had some trust issues that needed to be addressed. In the beginning I found it flattering that they always wanted to do everything with me, and was always concerned about what I was doing; the problems started however, when I decided to use my time more productively.

Again I must reiterate, I thought it was sweet so I was not initially concerned when I got the calls that said "Why don't you answer the phone when I call?" I started to make more of the effort to answer the phone when they called but, that also meant that I could not worship in my car anymore which I often do. When I did not address this behavior when it first began I was in essence condoning it, letting them think that this was okay when in reality it was not. When I finally decided to bring his trust issues to their attention, the conversation was immediately turned around to become my fault, and I was now accused of cheating. How can you defend yourself against something that you are not doing - YOU CANNOT! This is the same tactic that the enemy uses against us daily - he is the *accuser of the enemy*. Do not waste your time trying to reason with an individual who is an accuser for this is a losing battle.

Another area of concern lies in commitment. If you are more committed than the other individual to making the relationship work, no matter how beautiful the wedding is and how many well-wishers attended, it will not go well. You see, you will never agree on everything, and you may have more than a few shouting matches than others, but the thing which will keep you in the marriage itself is commitment. If they have a problem with commitment, you will eventually find yourself alone trying to figure out what happened, and what you could have done differently to make the relationship last; along with a broken heart and many, many, many tears. The answer to that question is "nothing". If they lack commitment, whether they walk away now or later makes no difference, they will walk away. The truth is that one cannot reason with anyone who is not committed. You cannot make anyone trust you, you cannot make anyone love you, and you certainly cannot make anyone stay with you if they do not want to be there. The only thing that you can do is be careful who you let into your inner courts. While I am not telling you to put up a guard to everyone who comes into your life, what I am telling you to do is to make sure that the Holy Spirit is the deciding factor on who you let in. By doing so, you can avoid the mistake of marrying the wrong person, and dealing with the emotional pain of being rejected by the one individual that you chose to love and cherish until death do you part. For once you get married the rules change. You no longer simply have the option of walking away if it is not working out. You now have the responsibility to try to find a way to make it work, and it you separate, try to reconcile first.

While many will say that divorce is not an option, that discussion is out the realm of this book. Therefore, I will leave that debate to those in the marriage ministry. What I will say is that it takes two people to make a relationship work. When you enter into a marriage covenant, be sure that after you have done all of the work to ensure that you are a suitable mate, and make sure that you do not waste it all on the individual who is not the right one.

Wisdom Key

"If you want a lifelong commitment then it is imperative that you also commit to giving it your all. Unless you complete this step, you are not only risking your happiness, but the happiness of your potential mate as well."

Chapter 13

Final Thoughts

The role of a spouse is more than just a position in a relationship. It is an office ordained by God and should not be taken lightly. If you are dating an individual who has this position filled by another, I would encourage you to rethink your decision. An individual who is having their needs fulfilled by another individual, does not have room in their life to develop a proper relationship with you. This is true for both men and women.

According to Genesis 2:24-25 a man is to leave his parents and cleave to his wife. This means that if a man whose life is still intertwined with his parents (or anyone else for that matter) will have a difficult time doing that. Worst yet, he may expect his wife to now take care of him like his parents did. Women, you may find yourself being compared to his mother, and given that you are not his mother you will not be able to meet his expectations. Another thing to consider is that she may not be willing to relinquish her role either. However, the message of leave and cleave is not just for men, it is for the women as well. The point here is that you are not to share your office with another, and you should not be expected to either. There are many women who still have not left daddy's home either, those who still have a sugar daddy. Men, you are not to compete with that! Before anyone can find the love that God intended for them, they must first give up on the childhood dream. True love moves beyond the illusion of love, and seeks to discover the true meaning of love. This cannot occur until all are willing to let go of the fabrications, ridding our minds of worldly programming, and then renewing and refilling our minds with the type of love that God truly intended. This cannot happen unless all parties have been introduced to and understand the love of Jesus Christ for themselves.

The kind of love I am talking about is agape love which is selfless, not self-centered and not self-seeking. The kind of love that I am talking about would cause one to lay down their lives for another. If you do not think that you could ever do something like that, then you are NOT ready! If you want a lifelong commitment then it is imperative that you also commit to giving it your all. Unless you complete this step, you are not only risking your happiness, but the happiness of your potential mate as well.

A confident individual knows what they are capable of, and this is often birthed out of their experiences and struggles. Sure one can learn from other people's challenges (and that is the preferred method) but let's face it experience is truly the greatest teacher. While we often shrug from people who had a lot of life challenges, an individual who has overcome a life of challenges and struggles is a rare jewel indeed. They have tasted of the bitterness of the world, and yet they have also risen to the occasion. This type of individual has experienced a lot, and learning from their struggles they did not allow it to overtake them. Yes, they are a precious and valuable jewel indeed, and this type of tenacity will come in handy when the challenges arise in the midst of their relationships. Should it not be embraced instead of cast off as rebellion and troublesome? Few individuals will take on the challenge and seek out the strength of such an individual, unaware of the benefits of having unearthed such a treasure.

The point of this book is to make sure that you not only know what to look for in a relationship, but you are to be absolutely sure that you are ready. Are you willing to do what you can to add to someone else's happiness and not subtract from it? Do you know what you want from a relationship? Do you know that your happiness is self-contained and not contingent on someone else's happiness? If your answers to those questions are "yes" and you have taken heed to the advice offered in this book to prepare yourself for a relationship, know that you can enter the dating world qualified, equipped, and confident that you are now ready to be successful. You are now activated and ready to participate in this stage of your life! I wish you the best.

Blessings and Happy Dating!

> *- Minister Karen*

References

Barton, D. (2004). Four Centuries of American Education. Aledo, TX, USA.

Everything Engagement. (n.d.). Retrieved on April 12, 2012 from http://www.everythingengagement.com/arranged-marriage-statistics.html

Maxwell, John (2007). *The Maxwell Leadership Bible*. Dallas, Texas: Thomas Nelson.

Merriam-Webster Online Dictionary. (2012).

Moreland, J. (2007). *Kingdom Triangle: Recover the Christian Mind, Renovate the Soul, Restore the Spirit's Power*. Grand Rapids: MI: Zondervan.

U.S. Department of Education. (n.d.). *IES National Center for Educational Statistics*.

Young, B. & Adams, S. (1999). *The 10 Commandments of Dating*. Nashville, TN: Thomas Nelson

Additional Books In Publication:

Are You Afraid of the Dark, Too?

Does It Pay To Obey?

Christian Dating: 20 Keys to Healthy Relationships

Look for these other books to come soon:

Hey, Do You Know My Friend?

Pearls of Wisdom for Relationships

The Deception of Spiritual Leadership

Copies of this and upcoming books are available from:

Mutual Blessings Books
Huntsville, AL
MBSuccess@karenmaloy.org
www.karenmaloy.org
315-657-3648

ABOUT THE AUTHOR

Karen Maloy is an Emotional Wellness Coach who helps individuals transition from emotional brokenness to emotional health. A great-grandmother now, Karen started her coaching business in 2006 to help other women emerge from an overwhelming life of past hurts while still running a household, raising children and even completing studies.

Karen Maloy has a passion for educating God's people according to biblical standards. Her message is that we must begin to link God's word and good practical common sense to have a strong healthy foundation. She asserts that unless we seek to educate our children according to God's biblical standards, we will continue to experience the decline we are experiencing in society - spiritually, morally and academically.

www.ingramcontent.com/pod-product-compliance
Lightning Source LLC
Chambersburg PA
CBHW070106070426
42448CB00038B/1827